# SCRUM!

Mark Woods and Ruth Owen

Consultant Sally Smith

Evans

First published in 2010
by Evans Brothers Limited
2A Portman Mansions
Chiltern Street
London W1U 6NR
UK

Printed in China by New Era Co. Ltd

British Library Cataloguing in Publication Data
Woods, Mark.
    Scrum!. -- (Top score)
    1. Mathematics--Juvenile literature. 2. Mathematics--
    Problems, exercises, etc.--Juvenile literature. 3. Rugby
    football--Juvenile literature.
    I. Title II. Series III. Owen, Ruth, 1967-
    510-dc22
    ISBN-13: 9780237542818

VISIT OUR WEBSITE
www.evansbooks.co.uk
Evans

*Developed & Created by* Ruby Tuesday Books Ltd

**Project Director** – Ruth Owen
**Designer** – Alix Wood
**Editor** – Ben Hubbard
**Consultants** – Sally Smith, Hilary Koll and Steve Mills
© Ruby Tuesday Books Limited 2010

## ACKNOWLEDGEMENTS

With thanks to the Year 5 and Year 6 students at St Cleer School, Liskeard, Cornwall for their invaluable feedback and help with the development of these books.

Images: Getty **front cover** (David Rogers), **7 top** (Chris Cusiter), **7 bottom** (Harry How), **8** (Scott Barbour), **9** (Jacques Demarthon), **10** (Harry How), **12** (Ross Land), **14** (David Rogers), **15** (Euan Murray), **16 top** (Simon Bruty), **16 centre** (Hulton Archive), **16 bottom, 17** (Phil Walter), **18** (Adrian Dennis), **19** (Jamie McDonald), **20** (David Rogers), **21** (David Rogers), **22** (Warren Little), **23** (Tom Shaw), **24** (Hannah Johnston), **25** (Hannah Johnston), **26–27** (Cameron Spencer), **28** (David Rogers), **29** (Jimmy Jeong); Shutterstock **title page**.

While every effort has been made to secure permission to use copyright material, the publishers apologise for any errors or omissions in the above list and would be grateful for notification of any corrections to be included in subsequent editions.

### MARK WOODS

Mark Woods is a sports journalist and regular BBC presenter and commentator. He writes on a variety of sports including football, basketball and rugby.

### RUTH OWEN

Ruth Owen is a children's non-fiction writer who has developed a number of innovative maths practice books.

### SALLY SMITH

Sally Smith has taught in primary, secondary and special schools and is currently a Leading Teacher for Maths. She has worked as a maths consultant for the Cornwall local authority.

# CONTENTS

THE POWER OF NUMBERS          6

RECORD BREAKERS              8

RUGBY – THE BASICS          10

THE BACKS                   12

THE FORWARDS                14

BLAST FROM THE PAST         16

NEIGHBOURS AND RIVALS       18

THE LIONS                   20

6 NATIONS                   22

THE ALL BLACKS              24

AUSTRALIA AND SOUTH AFRICA  26

THE WORLD CUP               28

ANSWERS                     30

# THE POWER OF NUMBERS

What does a Number 8 do? Should a team go for a try in the last minute or try to kick a drop goal? Who is at the top of the points table? Everywhere in rugby, numbers count.

Whether you are adding up the score or doing calculations to work out who is the best team in a league or competition, you need to do your sums.

We can even find out what position a player is on the field by looking at the number on the back of his or her jersey.

**To become a top rugby player takes practice. It's the same with numbers. When you practise your maths skills, you improve your maths fitness.**

There is a legend that rugby was invented at Rugby School in England in 1823. A pupil called William Webb Ellis decided to pick up a football in his hands and run with it. No one knows for sure if this story is true, but around this time rugby and football became two different sports with their own sets of rules.

*The New Zealand Black Ferns (in black) play Canada in the 2006 Women's Rugby World Cup.*

Chris Cusiter of Scotland releases the ball from the scrum.

## SCRUM

Sometimes, to decide who gets possession, players from each team push against each other in a big group to win the ball.

The first Women's Rugby World Cup was held in 1991. The Black Ferns of New Zealand have won the tournament three times.

Let's get started!

# RECORD BREAKERS

There have been some amazing games and achievements in rugby. Here are some record-breaking rugby facts and statistics.

**45**

Simon Culhane of New Zealand holds the record for the most points scored in a single World Cup game. He scored 45 points against Japan in 1995. Culhane's record-breaking points total included a try (five points) and 20 conversions (two points each).

**164**

In 1994, Hong Kong beat Singapore 164–13, the most points ever scored in a single international Test game. In 2002, Japan achieved the biggest ever winning margin when they beat Chinese Taipei 155–3.

**155**

**139**

George Gregan played for his national team more times than any other player. He made 139 international appearances for Australia between 1994 and 2007.

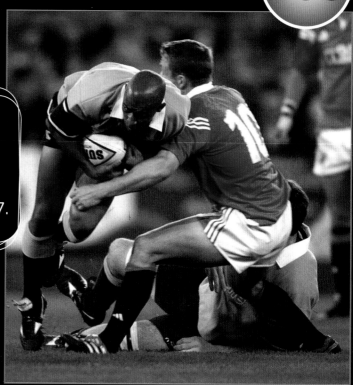

*Jonny Wilkinson tackles George Gregan (left) during a match between The British and Irish Lions and Australia in 2001.*

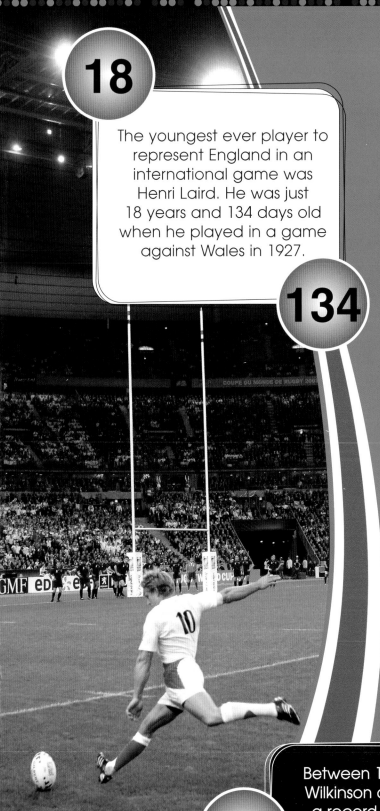

**18**

The youngest ever player to represent England in an international game was Henri Laird. He was just 18 years and 134 days old when he played in a game against Wales in 1927.

**134**

Jonny Wilkinson goes for a conversion.

**249**

Between 1999 and 2007, Jonny Wilkinson of England collected a record-breaking 249 points in World Cup games.

# RECORD BREAKERS QUIZ

Try these quiz questions using rugby's record-breaking numbers.

1) Write down the numbers in the red circles.
   a) Put the numbers in order starting with the smallest.
   b) Which numbers are odd and which are even?
   c) Round each of the numbers up or down to the nearest 10.

2) Hong Kong beat Singapore 164–13. What was the difference in the scores?

3) Try these calculations that use the numbers in the red circles.
   a) **139 + 45 =**     b) **164 – 155 =**
   c) **249 – 45 =**     d) **249 + 134 =**
   e) **18 + 45 =**      f)  **139 – 18 =**

4) Which of the numbers in the red circles are multiples of 9?

5) Henri Laird was 18 years and 134 days old when he first played for England. Can you give Henri's age in years, weeks and days?

# RUGBY – THE BASICS

There are two main types of rugby – union and league. In this book we will focus on rugby union. Players win points by scoring tries and by kicking the ball between the H-shaped goal posts.

## KNOW YOUR RUGBY

- A rugby union team is made up of eight forwards, numbered 1 to 8, and seven backs, numbered 9 to 15. Each player has a specific role in attack or defence.

- Teams move the ball forward by running with it or kicking it. Players can only pass the ball to each other backwards. The opposing side will try to tackle the player with the ball and push him or her to the ground.

- If the ball is thrown forward or gets trapped under a group of players, there is a scrum.

- When the ball goes out of play, one team must throw it back in. This is called a line-out.

- Top players play for their country in games known as Tests. For each appearance they earn a cap.

*The line-out*

10

## PLAYER POSITIONS GRID MAP
### This diagram shows the players' positions on the pitch.

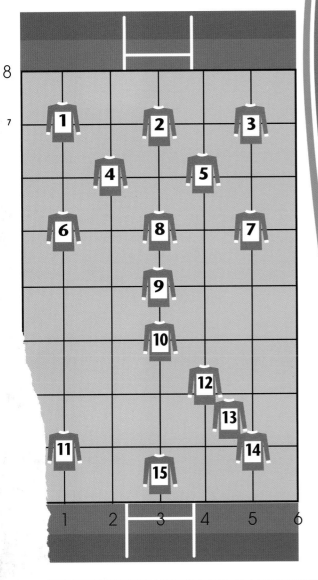

## RUGBY BASICS QUIZ

Try these quiz questions about playing rugby.

**1)** Read the **How To Score** box. How many points did each of these players earn?
   a) Jonny – 2 tries and 4 conversions.
   b) Bill – 3 drop goals, 1 try and 1 penalty.
   c) Alex – 3 tries, 2 drop goals and 1 conversion.

**2)** A team scores six tries and some conversions. If their final score is 40 points, how many conversions did they make?

**3)** A match lasts for 80 minutes. How many minutes did these team members play for?
   a) Carly played for half the game.
   b) Sam played for a quarter of the game.
   c) Becky played for $3/4$ of the game.

Look at the **Player Positions Grid Map**.

**4)** Which players are at these positions?
a) **(4,2)**  b) **(1,5)**  c) **(3,7)**  d) **(5,7)**

**5)** What are the grid positions of these players?
   a) 14   b) 7   c) 10   d) 1

## HOW TO SCORE

- **Tries** The ball is carried over the try line at the end of the field and touched onto the ground to earn five points.
- **Conversions** When a team scores a try they get a bonus kick at goal. If the ball goes over the crossbar and between the posts, they score two points.
- **Penalties** A bonus kick at goal (to score three points) when the other team has broken a rule.
- **Drop Goals** A special kick at goal from anywhere on the field to score three points.

11

# THE BACKS

The backs are the speedy stars of a rugby team. They are often the players who score tries. The backs' job is to move the ball down the pitch and avoid being tackled by the opposition.

## WHO DOES WHAT?

**Full-back (15)**: Catches long kicks down the field and gets the ball back in the other direction. Must also be able to tackle if the opposing side breaks through.

**Wings (11 and 14)**: The players who attempt to score tries most often.

**Centres (12 and 13)**: Pass the ball, tackle and defend.

**Half-backs**: The **fly-half (10)** and **scrum-half (9)** help organise attacks. They decide on tactics and start the passing after a scrum. The fly-half often takes the kicks.

**DAN CARTER**

Date of birth: 5th March, 1982
New Zealander
Position: Fly-half
New Zealand caps: 66
New Zealand points: 994

(Statistics up to 1st June, 2010)

*Dan made his first appearance for New Zealand at 21 years old. He scored 20 points in his first game! Dan's dad, Neville, played the same position and helped Dan train when he was a kid.*

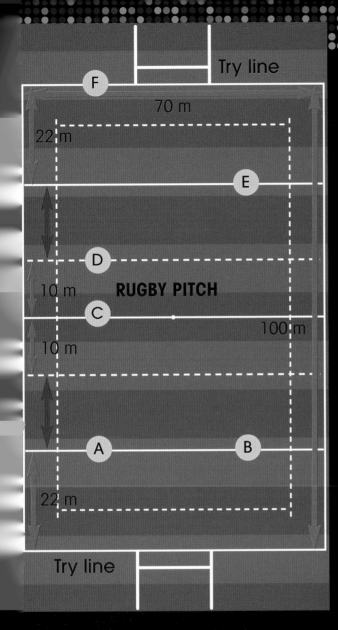

Try line

F

70 m

22 m

E

D

10 m    **RUGBY PITCH**

C

100 m

10 m

A          B

22 m

Try line

**JONNY WILKINSON**

**Date of birth:** 25th May, 1979
**English**
**Position:** Fly-half
**England caps:** 83
**England points:** 1172

(Statistics up to 1st June, 2010)

y Wilkinson is one of the most accurate
rs in rugby and has scored more
national points than any other player.

## BACKS QUIZ

Now try these quiz questions.

1) Use Dan and Jonny's facts to answer these quick questions.
   a) Who is the younger of the two players?
   b) If Dan plays for New Zealand 15 more times, how many caps will he have?
   c) What is the points difference between the two players?

Look at the **Rugby Pitch** diagram.

2) What is the perimeter of the pitch?

3) What is the area of the pitch?

4) How long are the sections marked with the blue arrows?

5) Try these questions about attacking moves using the diagram.
   a) Dan Carter kicks the ball from point A to point D. How long is the kick?
   b) Jonny Wilkinson runs from point B to point E. How far did he run?
   c) Jonny starts running with the ball from point B. He gets tackled to the ground at point D. How far from the try line is he?

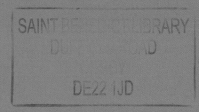

13

# THE FORWARDS

Rugby forwards are some of the biggest players in sport. Tough and powerful, they push and pull to help their side get the ball. Forwards take part in scrums and line-outs and stop the opposition by tackling them.

George Smith tackles Bryan Habana of South Africa.

## WHO DOES WHAT?

### FRONT ROW

- **Props (1 and 3)**: These heavy players provide the muscle to hold together the scrum and push the opposing side backwards.

- **Hooker (2)**: Tries to hook the ball to the back of the scrum with his or her feet. Leads the forwards in attack and defence.

- **Locks (4 and 5)**: The tallest players who try to jump up and win possession when the ball is thrown in from a line-out.

### BACK ROW

- **Flankers (6 and 7)**: These players tackle the opposition and take chances to attack.

- **Number 8**: A strong, athletic player who tries to create holes in the opposition's defence.

GEORGE SMITH

**Date of birth:** 14th July, 1980
**Australian**
**Position:** Flanker
**Height:** 1.8 m
**Weight:** 104 kg

*George Smith began playing for Australia before he'd played his first professional game. He earned 110 caps for Australia before he retired in 2010.*

14

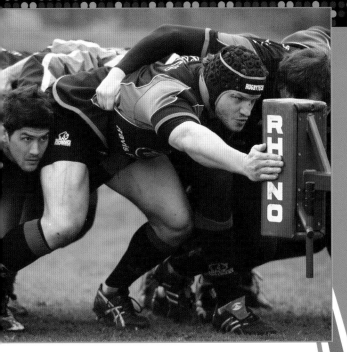

*Euan Murray (centre) practises his role in the scrum during a training session.*

## EUAN MURRAY

**Date of birth:** 7th August, 1980
**Scottish**
**Position:** Prop
**Height:** 1.85 m
**Weight:** 122 kg

*Euan Murray made his first appearance for Scotland at the age of 24. He has also played for The British and Irish Lions. Euan is not just a top rugby player, he's also a vet.*

# FORWARDS QUIZ

Try these quiz questions about rugby's biggest stars!

1) Use George and Euan's facts to answer these quick questions.
   a) What is the weight difference between George and Euan?
   b) What is their height difference? Give your answer in centimetres.

2) What is the age difference between the two players in days?

3) Look at these heights. Put them in order starting with the shortest.

   | 200 cm | 2.1 m | 1.85 m |
   |---|---|---|
   | 2150 mm | 195 cm | 1.89 m |

4) To become as strong as possible, forwards spend a lot of time in the gym lifting weights. Look at the weights on this barbell. How much will the player have to lift? Give your answer in kilograms.

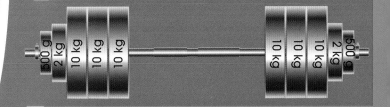

5) How much will the player have to lift if he adds the following additional weights to the barbells?
   a) 2 x **10 kg** and 2 x **5 kg**
   b) 2 x **5 kg** and 2 x **500 g**
   c) 2 x **15 kg**

# BLAST FROM THE PAST

Let's look at four of rugby union's greatest stars from the past.

## JONAH LOMU

Jonah Lomu had a huge impact at the 1995 World Cup. He had only played twice before for New Zealand. He scored seven tries in five matches.

## GARETH EDWARDS

Gareth Edwards became the youngest ever captain of Wales when he was 20. He was brilliant at passing and running. He later became a TV commentator.

**Date of birth:** 12th July, 1947
Welsh
**Position:** Scrum-half
**Height:** 1.73 m
**Weight:** 80 kg
**Points scored for Wales:** 88

**Date of birth:** 12th May, 1975
New Zealander
**Position:** Wing
**Height:** 1.96 m
**Weight:** 125 kg
**Points scored for New Zealand:** 185

## WILLIE JOHN MCBRIDE

Willie John McBride played on five Lions tours and made a record 17 Lions Test appearances. In 1974, he captained the Lions on a tour to South Africa. The Lions played 22 games. They had one draw and won the other 21 games!

**Date of birth:** 6th June, 1940
Irish
**Position:** Lock
**Height:** 1.91 m
**Weight:** 106 kg
**Points scored for Ireland:** 4

## MARTIN JOHNSON

**Date of birth:** 9th March, 1970
**English**
**Position:** Lock
**Height:** 2 m
**Weight:** 119 kg
**Points scored for England:** 10

*Martin Johnson became a hero of English rugby when he captained the team that won the 2003 World Cup. In 2008, he became the manager of England.*

# BLAST FROM THE PAST QUIZ

Try these quiz questions about some of rugby's top stars.

1) This pictogram shows how many times each player was capped for his country. How many caps did Martin Johnson earn?

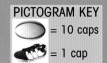

PICTOGRAM KEY
= 10 caps
= 1 cap

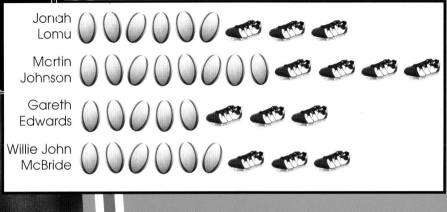

Jonah Lomu
Martin Johnson
Gareth Edwards
Willie John McBride

2) Which two players earned the same number of caps? How many?

3) Put the players in order according to their weight, starting with the heaviest.

4) What is the mean height of the players?

5) Each of these sequences starts with the number of points one of the players scored for his country. Can you fill in the gaps?
   a) **88   80   ?   64   56   ?   40**
   b) **4   8   ?   32   ?   128   ?**
   c) **185   180   ?   155   135   ?   80**
   d) **10   7   ?   1   −2   ?   −8**

# NEIGHBOURS AND RIVALS

In rugby union, the United Kingdom's four countries have separate teams. England, Wales and Scotland have their own sides. Northern Ireland and the Republic of Ireland combine to make a single Ireland team. Games between the four teams are very competitive!

The first ever international rugby match was played between Scotland and England in 1871. Scotland beat England 4–1.

*England (in white) and Wales in action during the 2010 Six Nations Competition.*

| STADIUMS | | | |
|---|---|---|---|
| Team | Stadium name | City | Capacity |
| England | Twickenham | London | 82,000 |
| Ireland | Aviva Stadium | Dublin | 50,000 |
| Scotland | Murrayfield | Edinburgh | 67,000 |
| Wales | Millennium Stadium | Cardiff | 74,500 |

## HEAD TO HEAD

| | Number of wins | | | Draws |
|---|---|---|---|---|
| England | 54 | 53 | Wales | 12 |
| England | 67 | 42 | Scotland | 18 |
| England | 70 | 45 | Ireland | 8 |
| Wales | 64 | 48 | Scotland | 3 |
| Wales | 62 | 47 | Ireland | 6 |
| Scotland | 64 | 55 | Ireland | 5 |

(Statistics up to 1st May, 2010)

*Ireland (in green) and Scotland in action during the 2008 Six Nations competition.*

Ireland's biggest win over Scotland was in 2000. The score was 44–22. In 1997, Scotland beat Ireland 38–10.

# UK TEAMS QUIZ

**Answer these quiz questions.**

The **Head to Head** table on this page shows the results of games between the UK teams. For example, England has beaten Wales 54 times. Wales has beaten England 53 times. The two teams have drawn 12 times.

1) How many times has Scotland played Ireland?

2) Which of the four teams has won the most head to head games? How many?

3) How many draws has Ireland had in head to head games?

4) England are playing Wales at the Millennium Stadium. There are 34,600 England fans and 41,500 Wales fans trying to buy tickets. How many fans won't get a ticket?

5) This table shows the all-time Test records for the four teams. Can you fill in the missing numbers?

| TEST RECORDS (to end 2009) | | | | |
|---|---|---|---|---|
| | Played | Won | Lost | Drawn |
| England | 620 | | 244 | 48 |
| Wales | 608 | 315 | 265 | |
| Scotland | | 242 | 300 | 32 |
| Ireland | 586 | 245 | | 29 |

# THE LIONS

The British and Irish Lions are a special team made up of the best players from England, Wales, Scotland and Ireland.

| 2009 LIONS TOUR CLUB GAMES RESULTS | | | |
|---|---|---|---|
| Opponents | Score | Lions | Points difference |
| Royal XV | 37–25 | Lions | 12 |
| Golden Lions | 10-74 | Lions | 64 |
| Free State Cheetahs | 24-26 | Lions | |
| Natal Sharks | 3-39 | Lions | |
| Western Province | 23-26 | Lions | |
| Southern Kings | 8-20 | Lions | |
| Emerging Springboks | 13-13 | Lions | |

## THE LIONS ON TOUR

- The Lions organise a tour every four years to either Australia, New Zealand or South Africa. They play a series of games against club and international sides.

- The tours last for up to two months. Thousands of fans travel with the team to cheer them on.

- Sometimes the Lions play a special match in another country such as France or Argentina.

*The Lions (in red) tackle Wynard Olivier of South Africa during the third Test match in 2009.*

# THE LIONS QUIZ

Try these quiz questions about the Lions.

1) The Lions play South Africa 46 times. They lose 23 games and draw six times. How many times do the Lions beat South Africa?

2) The Lions play New Zealand 38 times. They lose 29 times. How many times do the Lions beat New Zealand if they win twice as many games as they draw?

3) In 2009, the Lions toured South Africa. Look at the **2009 Lions Tour Club Games Results** table. Complete the points difference column of the table.

Now look at the **First Test** table. It shows what happened in the first Test between the Lions and South Africa in 2009. The table shows which players scored. It also shows in what minute of the game each player scored.

4) How many points did each team score?

5) The first Test began at 3:00 pm.
   a) At what time did Pienaar score his second penalty?

   The first half lasted 40 minutes. Then there were 10 minutes of half-time.

   b) At what time did Brussow score his try?
   c) At what time did Croft score his second try?

*Tom Croft of the Lions dives for his second try during the first Test match between the Lions and South Africa in 2009.*

| FIRST TEST | | | | |
|---|---|---|---|---|
| Player | Tries<br>5 points | Conversions<br>2 points | Penalties<br>3 points | Minute<br>of game |
| **South Africa** | | | | |
| Smit | 1 | | | 5 |
| Brussow | 1 | | | 46 |
| Pienaar | | 2 | | |
| Pienaar | | | 3 | 11,32,35 |
| F. Steyn | | | 1 | 20 |
| **Lions** | | | | |
| Croft | 2 | | | 22,67 |
| Phillips | 1 | | | 74 |
| S. Jones | | 3 | | |

21

# 6 NATIONS

Every spring, England, Scotland, Wales, Ireland, France and Italy play each other in a tournament called the 6 Nations. There is a men's 6 Nations and a women's competition. Every team plays one game against each of the other five teams.

If a team wins all five of their games they earn the "Grand Slam". The team that finishes last is said to have won the "wooden spoon".

England captain Catherine Spencer poses with the 6 Nations trophy that the team won in 2009.

**11**

The England women's team have won the 6 Nations more times than any other team. In 2010, they won for the 11th time.

**80**

In 2001, England scored 80 points against Italy. That's the highest ever score in the competition.

| MEN'S 6 NATIONS ALL-TIME STATS | | | | | | |
|---|---|---|---|---|---|---|
| | England | Wales | France | Scotland | Ireland | Italy |
| Tournaments | 110 | 110 | 80 | 110 | 110 | 11 |
| Wins | 25 | 24 | 17 | 14 | 11 | 0 |
| Shared Wins | 10 | 11 | 8 | 8 | 8 | 0 |
| Grand Slams | 12 | 10 | 9 | 3 | 2 | 0 |

(Statistics up to and including 2010 Six Nations)

*Scotland versus Wales in 2010*

# 6 NATIONS QUIZ

Try these 6 Nations quiz questions.

1) By 2010, the England men's team had won 12 Grand Slams. List all the factors of 12.

2) In 2010, France had played in the 6 Nations tournament 80 times. How many fours are there in 80?

3) England has won the 6 Nations 25 times. Which of these numbers are multiples of 25?
   **50   105   125   75   205**

4) Look at the **6 Nations Results 2010** table. Which game had the biggest points difference?

We can use a table like the one below to show a competition's results. We've filled out the results for England in the 2010 6 Nations.

| 6 NATIONS RESULTS 2010 | | |
|---|---|---|
| **WEEK 1** | | |
| Ireland | 29-11 | Italy |
| England | 30-17 | Wales |
| Scotland | 9-18 | France |
| **WEEK 2** | | |
| Wales | 31-24 | Scotland |
| France | 33-10 | Ireland |
| Italy | 12-17 | England |
| **WEEK 3** | | |
| Wales | 20-26 | France |
| Italy | 16-12 | Scotland |
| England | 16-20 | Ireland |
| **WEEK 4** | | |
| Ireland | 27-12 | Wales |
| Scotland | 15-15 | England |
| France | 46-20 | Italy |
| **WEEK 5** | | |
| Wales | 33-10 | Italy |
| Ireland | 20-23 | Scotland |
| France | 12-10 | England |

|  | Played | Games won | Draws | Games lost | Points | Match points for | Match points against | Points difference |
|---|---|---|---|---|---|---|---|---|
| England | 5 | 2 | 1 | 2 | 5 | 88 | 76 | +12 |
| France |  |  |  |  |  |  |  |  |
| Ireland |  |  |  |  |  |  |  |  |
| Italy |  |  |  |  |  |  |  |  |
| Scotland |  |  |  |  |  |  |  |  |
| Wales |  |  |  |  |  |  |  |  |

**Win = 2 points        Draw = 1 point**

5) Now draw the table and fill out the results for the other 5 teams.

# THE ALL BLACKS

The New Zealand All Blacks are the fiercest, toughest and most successful Test team in history. Their black jersey with a silver fern is known all around the world. It has been worn since the team's first match in 1884.

*The All Blacks perform a traditional Maori dance called the Haka before every game. They perform the dance in front of their opponents. The Haka is designed to show off the team's strength and scare the other side!*

| ALL BLACKS TEST RECORDS | | | | |
|---|---|---|---|---|
| OPPONENT | PLAYED | WON | LOST | DRAWN |
| Argentina | 13 | 12 | 0 | 1 |
| Australia | 136 | | 39 | 5 |
| British & Irish Lions | 38 | 29 | 6 | |
| Canada | 4 | 4 | 0 | 0 |
| England | 33 | 26 | | 1 |
| Fiji | 4 | 4 | 0 | 0 |
| France | 49 | 36 | 12 | 1 |
| Ireland | 22 | 21 | 0 | 1 |
| Italy | 11 | 11 | 0 | 0 |
| Japan | 1 | 1 | 0 | 0 |
| Pacific Islanders | 1 | 1 | 0 | 0 |
| Portugal | 1 | 1 | 0 | 0 |
| Romania | 2 | 2 | 0 | 0 |
| Samoa | 5 | 5 | 0 | 0 |
| Scotland | | 25 | 0 | 2 |
| South Africa | 78 | 42 | | 3 |
| Tonga | 3 | 3 | 0 | 0 |
| USA | 2 | 2 | 0 | 0 |
| Wales | 25 | 22 | 3 | 0 |
| World XV | 3 | 2 | 1 | 0 |
| TOTAL | | | | |

(Statistics up to 1st May, 2010)

**1711** points

**232** tries

The All Blacks won the first World Cup in 1987. They have scored more World Cup points and tries than any other country.

*The All Blacks win a line-out against France.*

# ALL BLACKS QUIZ

Answer these quiz questions about the All Blacks.

1) Look at the **All Blacks Test Records** table. Fill in the yellow gaps.

2) Now add up the totals for each column. How many Test games have the All Blacks played, won, lost and drawn?

3) Give the following ratios in their simplest forms:
   a) What ratio of wins to losses do the All Blacks have against France?
   b) What ratio of wins to draws do the All Blacks have against South Africa?

4) The All Blacks have scored an amazing **1711 points** in World Cup games.
   a) What is the number **7** worth in this number?
   b) What is the biggest number we can make using **1, 7, 1** and **1**?

5) In 1995, the All Blacks beat Japan **145–17**. It was the biggest World Cup win ever. On page 11 we looked at how points are scored in a rugby game. How many different ways can you find to score **145 points**?

# AUSTRALIA AND SOUTH AFRICA

Rocky Elsom of Australia breaks through South Africa's defence in the 2009 Tri-Nations.

Australia and South Africa are two powerful Test teams. Every year the two teams compete with New Zealand in the Tri-Nations. The three countries' top clubs also play each other in a league competition called the Super 14.

| TRI-NATIONS RESULTS | | | | | | | | |
|---|---|---|---|---|---|---|---|---|
| | Pld | W | L | D | Titles | Points for | Points against | Points difference |
| New Zealand | 62 | 42 | 20 | 0 | 9 | 1657 | 1220 | +437 |
| South Africa | 62 | 26 | 35 | 1 | 3 | 1279 | 1539 | −260 |
| Australia | 62 | 24 | 37 | 1 | 2 | 1277 | 1454 | −177 |

(Statistics up to and Including 2009 Tri-Nations)

The Tri-Nations tournament started in 1996. New Zealand has won nine titles.

The South African team are known as the Springboks. Rugby is hugely popular in South Africa with every game being shown on TV. The Springboks won the Rugby World Cup in 1995 and 2007.

The Australian team are known as the Wallabies. They won the World Cup in 1991 and 1999.

## AUSTRALIA AND SOUTH AFRICA QUIZ

Now try these quiz questions.

1) In head to head games Australia has won 26 times. South Africa has won 40 times. The two teams have drawn once. How many times have the two teams played each other?

2) In the Tri-Nations competition the three teams all play each other three times. How many games are there in the tournament?

3) If a ticket to a Tri-Nations game costs $125, how much will it cost to buy three tickets for three games?

4) Look at the **Tri-Nations Results** table. Some teams have a negative points difference. They've had more points scored against them than they have scored. Calculate the negative points difference for the teams below.

| | Points for | Points against | Difference |
|---|---|---|---|
| TEAM A | 60 | 70 | |
| TEAM B | 37 | 42 | |
| TEAM C | 100 | 120 | |
| TEAM D | 67 | 83 | |

5) Using the **Tri-Nations Results** table answer true or false to these statements.
a) Australia has won over one third of its games.
b) New Zealand has lost about a third of its games.
c) South Africa has won more than 50% of its games.
d) New Zealand has won two thirds of its games.

# THE WORLD CUP

| WORLD CUP WINNERS | |
| --- | --- |
| **MEN'S** | |
| 1987 | New Zealand |
| 1991 | Australia |
| 1995 | South Africa |
| 1999 | Australia |
| 2003 | England |
| 2007 | South Africa |
| **WOMEN'S** | |
| 1991 | USA |
| 1994 | England |
| 1998 | New Zealand |
| 2002 | New Zealand |
| 2006 | New Zealand |

The Rugby World Cup is the biggest competition in rugby union. Every four years 20 international teams compete. The World Cup began in 1987. The All Blacks were the first winners of the World Cup.

**22**

Jason Leonard of England has the record for the most World Cup appearances. He played 22 times between 1991 and 2003.

**6**

All Black Marc Ellis holds the record for the most tries in a single World Cup game. He scored six tries against Japan in 1995.

**126**

Grant Fox of New Zealand has the record for the most points scored by a player in a single World Cup competition. He scored 126 points in 1987.

Jason Leonard of England in action in the 2003 World Cup.

# WORLD CUP QUIZ

Finally, try these quiz questions.

1) Mark Ellis scored six tries in a single World Cup game. If a try is worth five points, how many points did he add to his team's total?

2) What number can be added to 126 to make 200?

3) Using the numbers **6, 22** and **126** make as many addition and subtraction sums as you can in two minutes. Here's one to get you started:
**126 + 6 − 22 =**

4) Look at the **World Cup Winners** table.
   a) In what years will the next five Men's World Cups be held?
   b) The Women's World Cup is now held every four years. In what years will the next five Women's World Cups be held?

5) In rugby the players can only pass backwards. It's important they get the angle of their pass just right. Look at the **Rugby Passes** diagrams. Player number 10 is passing to number 14. What angles do passes A, B and C make?

*Amiria Marsh of New Zealand tries to pass the ball during the 2006 Women's World Cup Final between New Zealand and England. New Zealand won 25–17.*

## RUGBY PASSES

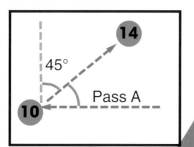

45°
Pass A

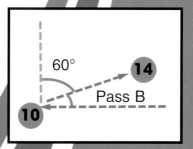

60°
Pass B

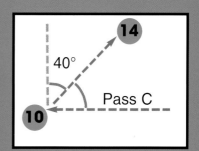

40°
Pass C

29

## 9 RECORD BREAKERS QUIZ

1. a) 18  45  134  139  155  164  249
   b) Odd = 45, 139, 155, 249
      Even = 18, 134, 164
   c) 20, 50, 130, 140, 160, 160, 250
2. 151
3. a) 139 + 45 = 184
   b) 164 – 155 = 9
   c) 249 – 45 = 204
   d) 249 + 134 = 383
   e) 18 + 45 = 63
   f) 139 – 18 = 121
4. 18  45
5. 18 years, 19 weeks, 1 day

## 11 RUGBY BASICS QUIZ

1. a) 18  b) 17  c) 23
2. 5 conversions
3. a) 40 minutes  b) 20 minutes
   c) 60 minutes
4. a) 12  b) 6  c) 2  d) 3
5. a) **(5,1)**  b) **(5,5)**
   c) **(3,3)**  d) **(1,7)**

## 13 BACKS QUIZ

1. a) Dan Carter  b) 81  c) 178
2. 340 m
3. 7000 sq m
4. 18 m
5. a) 38 m  b) 56 m  c) 40 m

## 15 FORWARDS QUIZ

1. a) 18 kg  b) 5 cm
2. 24 days
3. 1.85 m  1.89 m  195 cm
   200 cm  2.1 m  2150 mm
4. 65 kg
5. a) 95 kg  b) 76 kg  c) 95 kg

## 17 BLAST FROM THE PAST QUIZ

1. 84 caps
2. Jonah Lomu and Willie John McBride 63 caps

3. Jonah Lomu; Martin Johnson; Willie John McBride; Gareth Edwards
4. 1.9 m
5. a) 72, 48  b) 16, 64, 256
   c) 170, 110  d) 4, –5

## 19 UK TEAMS QUIZ

1. 124
2. England 191 games
3. 19 draws   4 1600 fans
5. England won 328
   Wales drawn 28
   Scotland played 574
   Ireland lost 312

## 21 THE LIONS QUIZ

1. 17    2 6
3. Free State Cheetahs/Lions 2
   Natal Sharks/Lions 36
   Western Province/Lions 3
   Southern Kings/Lions 12
   Emerging Springboks/Lions 0
4. South Africa 26; the Lions 21
5. a) 3:32 pm  b) 3:56 pm
   c) 4:17 pm

## 23 6 NATIONS QUIZ

1. 1, 2, 3, 4, 6, 12
2. 20
3. 50, 125, 75
4. France v Italy 46-20
5. Your table should look like the table below.

## 25 ALL BLACKS QUIZ

1. Australia won 92
   British & Irish Lions drawn 3
   England lost 6
   Scotland played 27
   South Africa lost 33
2. The column totals are as follows:
   Played 458     Won 341
   Lost 100      Drawn 17
3. a) 3:1  b) 14:1
4. a) 700  b) 7111

## 27 AUSTRALIA AND SOUTH AFRICA QUIZ

1. 67   2 9   3 $1125
4. Team A  –10
   Team B  –5
   Team C  –20
   Team D  –16
5. a) True  b) True  c) False
   d) True

## 29 WORLD CUP QUIZ

1. 30
2. 74
3. 126 + 6 – 22 = 110
4. Men's     Women's
   2011      2010
   2015      2014
   2019      2018
   2023      2022
   2027      2026
5. Pass A 45°
   Pass B 30°
   Pass C 50°

| | Played | Games won | Draws | Games lost | Points | Match points for | Match points against | Points difference |
|---|---|---|---|---|---|---|---|---|
| England | 5 | 2 | 1 | 2 | 5 | 88 | 76 | +12 |
| France | 5 | 5 | 0 | 0 | 10 | 135 | 69 | +66 |
| Ireland | 5 | 3 | 0 | 2 | 6 | 106 | 95 | +11 |
| Italy | 5 | 1 | 0 | 4 | 2 | 69 | 137 | –68 |
| Scotland | 5 | 1 | 1 | 3 | 3 | 83 | 100 | –17 |
| Wales | 5 | 2 | 0 | 3 | 4 | 113 | 117 | –4 |